KEITH URBAN
DEFYING gravity

Contents

This book was approved by Keith Urban

Cover photo by Danny Clinch

Piano/vocal arrangements by John Nicholas

Cherry Lane Music Company
Director of Publications/Project Editor: Mark Phillips
Project Coordinator: Rebecca Skidmore

ISBN 978-1-60378-159-6

Visit our website at www.cherrylaneprint.com

MAX VADUKAL

On *Defying Gravity*, the openhearted and uplifting new album by Keith Urban, there is a deeply felt musical statement, a song cycle marked by a clearheaded sense of passion and hope. From the opening romantic yearning of "Kiss a Girl" to the heartfelt gratitude of the closing "Thank You," *Defying Gravity* offers listeners the inspiring and stirring sound of a great musical artist coming of age and creating his most personal and effecting music yet.

"Fortunately, this is where I am at right now in life, in my marriage, and in my home with a new girl," Urban says of *Defying Gravity's* truly joyful and thankful mood. "And coming down the road that I've taken to be here, I *do* feel a lot of gratitude."

The road that Keith Urban has traveled to get here has been uniquely his own. How else on earth to explain how this kid, born in Whangarie, New Zealand, and raised in Caboolture, Queensland, Australia, has grown up to somehow become one of the biggest stars in the very American world of Country music?

Since first moving to Nashville back in 1992, Keith Urban has gradually established himself as an extraordinary singer, songwriter, guitarist, and performer who has brought his own distinctive talent, energy, and charisma to Country music and beyond. In return, Urban has now established himself as both a global superstar and a highly respected artist with the impressive track record to prove it, including Grammy Awards, Country Music Association Awards, Academy of County Music Awards, and Australia's coveted Aria Award. He has a loyally devoted worldwide fan base that comes to see him every time he takes the stage, as he connects with the people who have made it all possible.

Keith Urban's millions of fans have followed his creative progression from his first American album as a member of the Ranch (1997), through an increasingly accomplished series of platinum-selling solo albums: *Keith Urban* (1999), *Golden Road* (2002), *Be Here* (2004), and *Love, Pain & the whole crazy thing* (2006), as well as the compilation *Greatest Hits: 19 Kids* (2008).

And so for a decade now, Urban has remained a welcome and enduring presence on Country radio thanks to a series of popular and memorable songs, including such No. 1 hits as "But for the Grace of God," "Somebody Like You," "Who Wouldn't Wanna Be Me," "You'll Think of Me," "Days Go By," "Making Memories of Us," "Better Life," "You Look Good in My Shirt" and "Start a Band," Urban's 2008 guitar and vocal duet with

2

pal Brad Paisley. And as a core artist on all Country video outlets, Urban's career to date has also been documented on a series of platinum video collections.

In recent years, Urban's remarkable musical gifts have also brought him to numerous places where Country superstars have rarely gone before, whether powerfully dueting with Alicia Keys on the Rolling Stones' "Gimme Shelter" on the stage of Live Earth, appearing on *Saturday Night Live*, or sitting in with the likes of Al Green, Justin Timberlake, B.B. King, and John Mayer at this year's Grammy Awards.

"I have a real appreciation for the long, colorful, diverse musical road I've taken to get here," Urban explains of his musical journey. "All through my youth in Australia, I got to play in so many different situations.

"You can't blame gravity for falling in love."
—Albert Einstein

I grew up in Tamworth—which is sort of the Country music capital of Australia—playing and competing there, but I also formed my own band playing West Coast Rock stuff that I loved. Then I got a job as a musical director for a cabaret singer, so I was learning "Twelfth of Never" and "Viva Las Vegas" too. At 16, I had to wear a tuxedo and count off the band. You name it—I played it in every pub and club in Australia, and that's given me a great palette to draw upon. I feel very lucky to have all these opportunities to play with so many artists who I really admire. Playing with people—and playing for people—is what it's all about."

For all the success and the close relationship he has made with his fans, the road that Keith Urban has taken has not been without its bumps, which only makes the happiness and peace that Urban has finally found in his own life—a subject he explores musically on *Defying Gravity*—all the more meaningful. Produced by Urban and Dann Huff, another gifted guitarist and longtime collaborator, *Defying Gravity* looks from a variety of perspectives at love as a life-saving, ever-changing force in our lives, from the excitement of courting on a song like "Sweet Thing," to the atmospheric heartbreak of "'Til Summer Comes Around," to the pure desire of "Standing Right in Front of You," to the constant longing for a love on "Why's It Feel So Long."

As Urban explains, "It wasn't a conscious theme, but listening back, I think the album is about being brave enough to love, which is difficult for a lot of people to do. Most people who have loved have been hurt, and to love for a second or third time is very, very hard. The tendency is to want to protect and pull back, but that's the very thing we *can't* do."

With *Defying Gravity,* Urban is bravely putting his passion, musical and otherwise, on the line as never before. As he explains, "Between marriage and sobriety and having a child, it's been an extraordinary gift that I just couldn't have imagined—or maybe I *could* have imagined but didn't know how, or when…or if. So, for those things to come together now is absolutely beautiful. It's allowed me to be present in a way I've never quite been. I was always thinking about tomorrow, or the past—anywhere but *here*. Even though I made an album called *Be Here*, I still wasn't ever *really* here. Now I love being present—I have a lot to be grateful for in the present."

Listen closely to *Defying Gravity*—gratitude has rarely sounded so good.

Kiss a Girl

Words and Music by
Monty Powell and Keith Urban

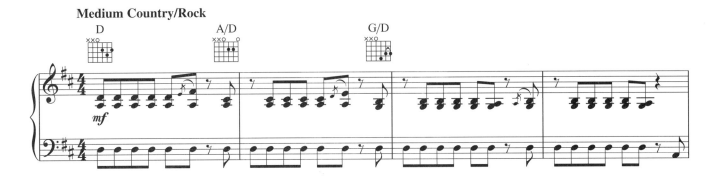

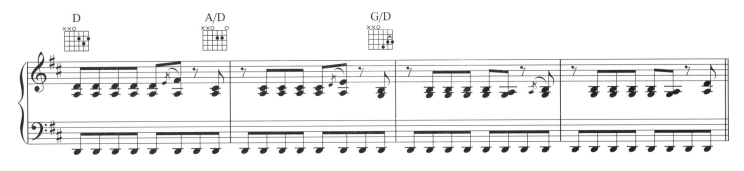

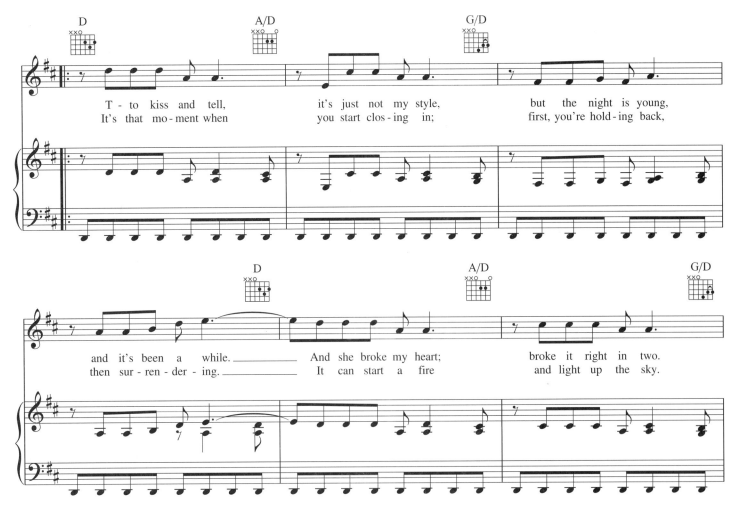

Lyrics:

T - to kiss and tell, it's just not my style, but the night is young,
It's that mo - ment when you start clos - ing in; first, you're hold - ing back,

and it's been a while. ___ And she broke my heart; broke it right in two.
then sur - ren - der - ing. ___ It can start a fire and light up the sky.

And it took some time, but I'm feel-ing like I'm _____ fi-n'lly read-

Such a sim-ple thing. Do you wan-na try? _____ Are you read-

y to find, _____ find some-bod-y new. _____

y to say good-bye _____ to all ____ these rules? _____

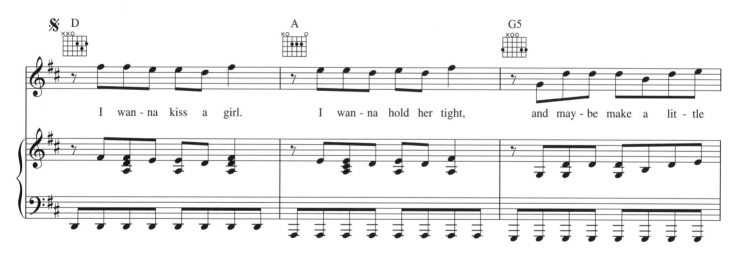

I wan-na kiss a girl. I wan-na hold her tight, and may-be make a lit-tle

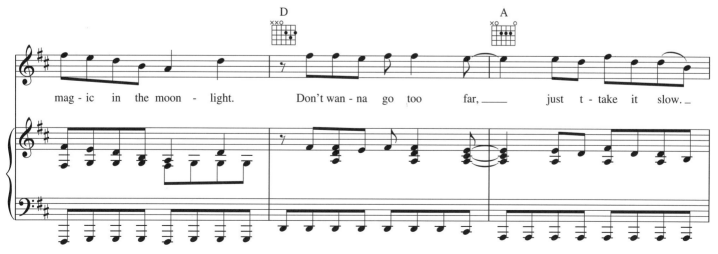

mag-ic in the moon-light. Don't wan-na go too far, ____ just t-take it slow. _

But I should-n't be lone - ly in this big ol' world. _

I _ wan - na kiss a girl.

Ooh.

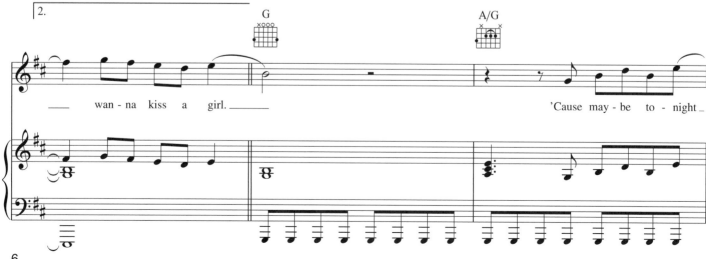

_ wan - na kiss a girl. _

'Cause may - be to - night _

it could turn _____ in - to the rest ___ of our _____

___ lives. _____ Oh, yeah. ___ Are you read - y? ___ Are you read -
(Are you read - y?

y _____ to cross ___ that __ line, _ put your lips ___ on mine? _____
Are you read - y?)

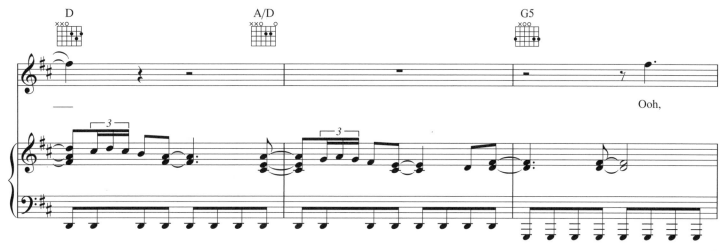

___ Ooh,

put your lips ___ on mine, ___ ba - by.

Do you wan - na try? ___ Are you read -

y to say good - bye ___ to all ___ these rules? ___

___ I wan - na kiss a girl. I wan - na hold her tight, ___

and may - be make a lit - tle mag - ic, ba - by. Don't wan - na go too far,

D   A/C#

D.S. al Coda

Bm   G   A

just to take it slow. But no one should be lone - ly. I should - n't be lone - ly.

Coda

A   G5   D   A/D

I wan - na kiss a girl. Na na na na na na. Na

G/D

na na na na na. Na Na na na na na. Na na na na na na.
I said I wan - na kiss a girl.

9

If Ever I Could Love

Words and Music by
Darrell Brown and Keith Urban

Moderately

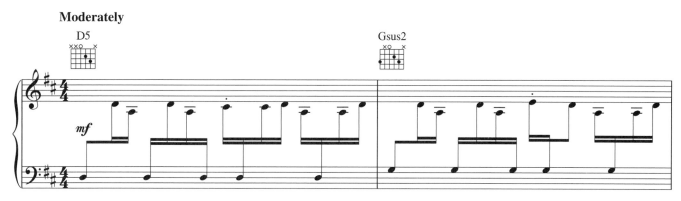

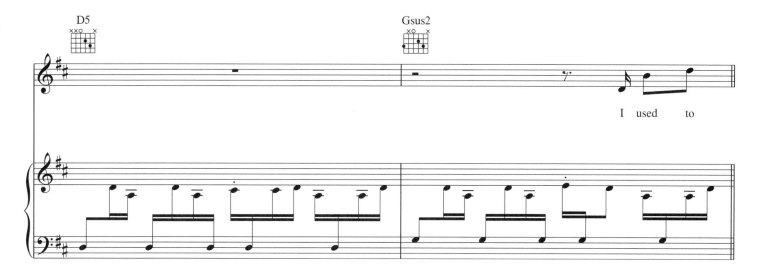

I used to

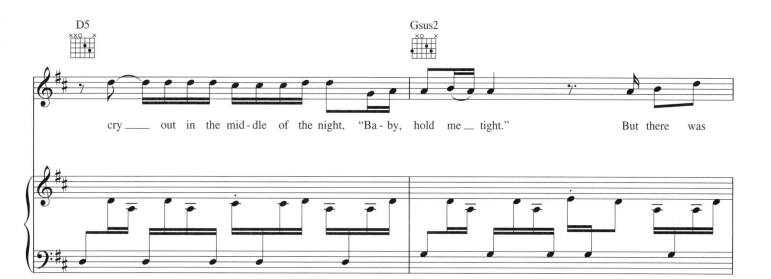

cry ___ out in the mid-dle of the night, "Ba-by, hold me ___ tight." But there was

no - bod - y be - side ___ me when I o - pened my eyes.

Now I've turned a cor - ner on ___ those days ___ and nights.

And some - thing in - side ___ me is chang - ing. I think I ___ might be start - ing

o - ver, ___ and I don't wan - na run.

Oh, no, _____ 'cause you might be __ the one, _____ ba - by.

If ev - er I could love, I think it could be with you.

If ev - er I thought I _____ found some - bod - y so true, __

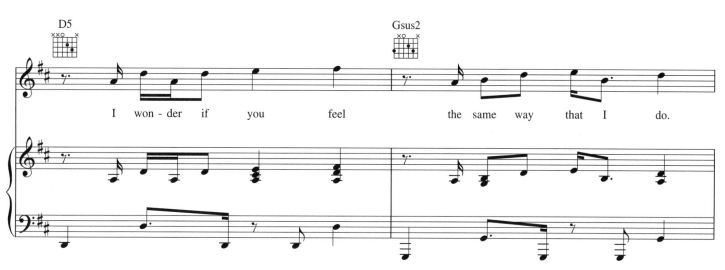

I won - der if you feel the same way that I do.

If ev-er I could love, I think it could be with you.

You know, I

can't read your mind, __ my love, but it seems __ to me __

that your heart and mine ___ to-night ___ are de-fy-ing grav-i-ty.

There's some-thing so ___ fa-mil-iar and still so un-known. ___

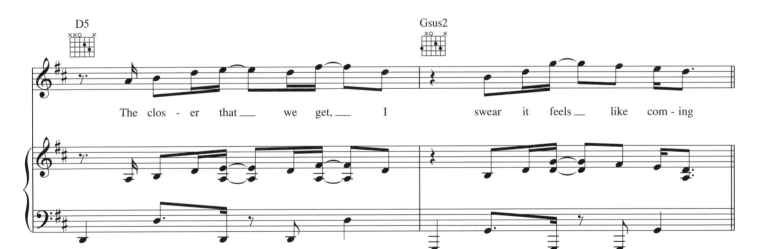

The clos-er that ___ we get, ___ I swear it feels ___ like com-ing

home. _____ I'm read-y to be brave. ___

Oh, yeah, _____ then you look at me and say. ba - by:

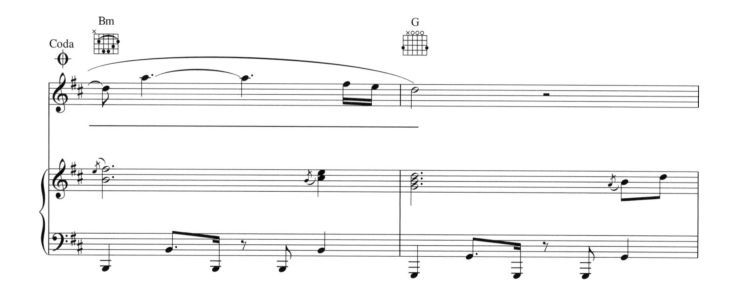

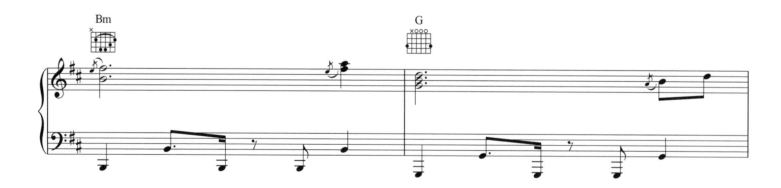

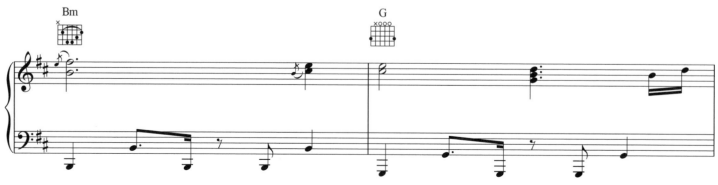

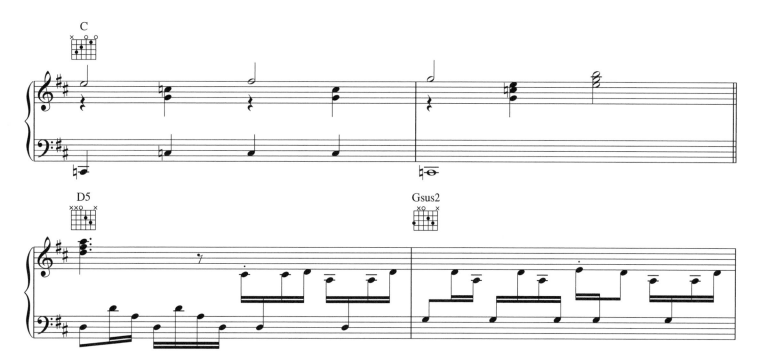

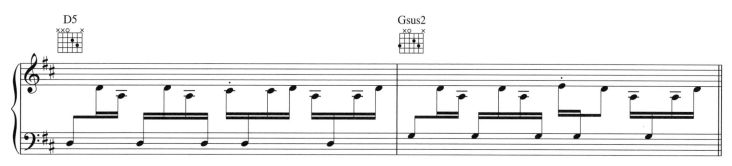

If ev-er I could love, oh, ba - by.

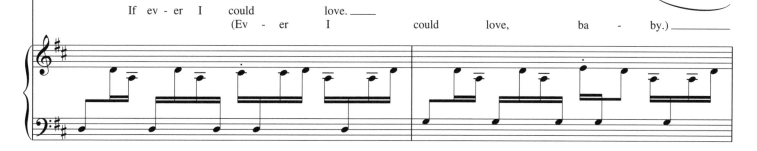

If ev-er I could love. ____
(Ev - er I could love, ba - by.) ____

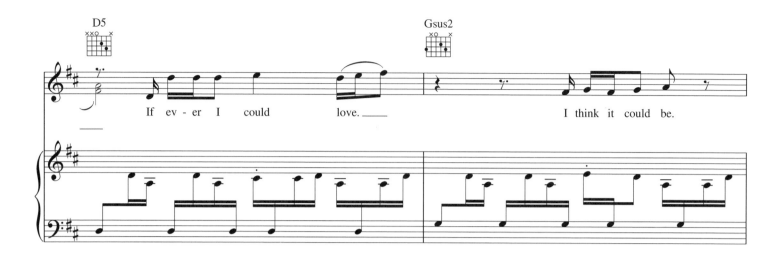

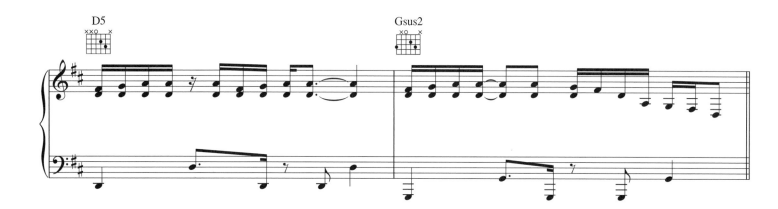

Repeat and fade

Sweet Thing

Words and Music by
Monty Powell and Keith Urban

Moderate Country/Rock

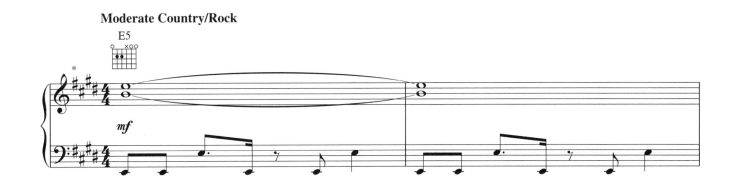

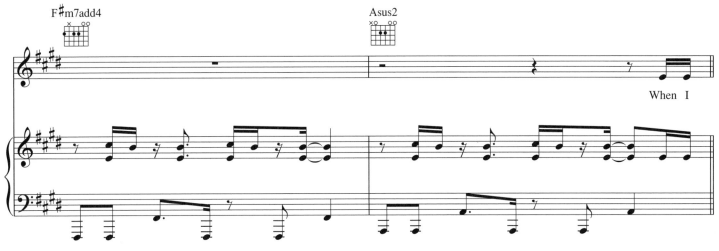

When I

*Recorded a half step lower.

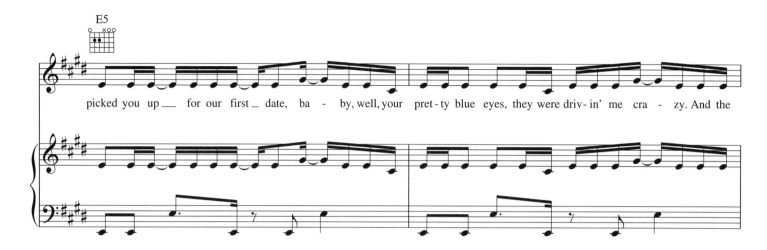

picked you up __ for our first __ date, ba - by, well, your pret - ty blue eyes, they were driv - in' me cra - zy. And the

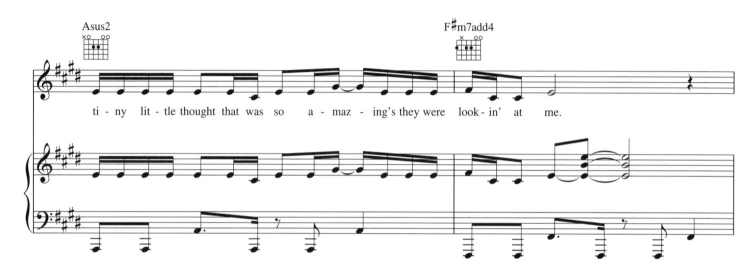

ti - ny lit - tle thought that was so a - maz - ing's they were look - in' at me.

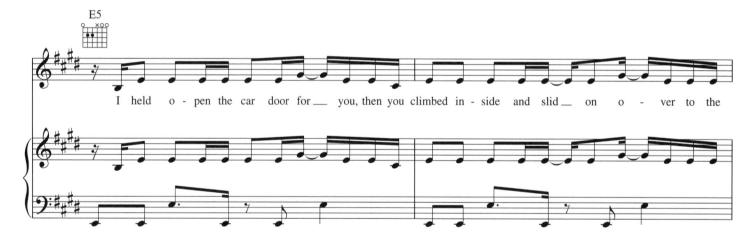

I held o - pen the car door for __ you, then you climbed in - side and slid __ on o - ver to the

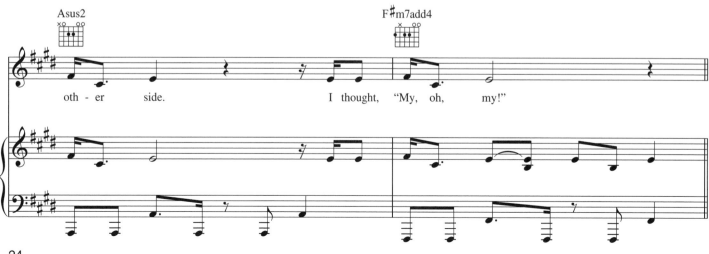

oth - er side. I thought, "My, oh, my!"

Sweet thing, the moon is high __ and the night is young. __ Come on and

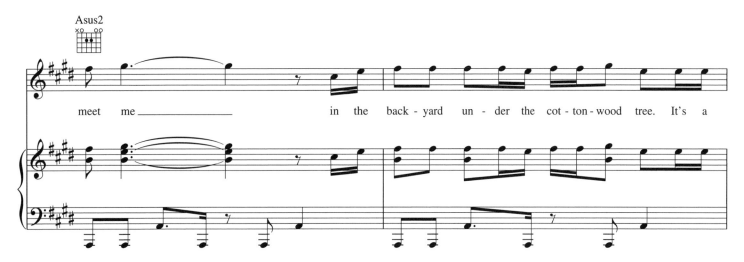

meet me _____ in the back-yard un-der the cot-ton-wood tree. It's a

good __ thing. Am I wish-in'? _____ Oh, come on,

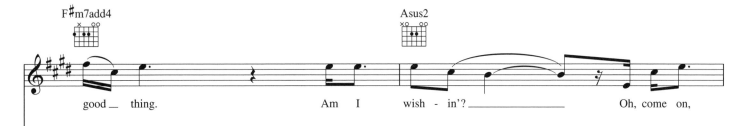

sweet thing. Oh, won't you climb on out __ of your win-dow while __ the world's

sleep - ing.   You know I need___ you and there's no way I'll be

leav - in'   till we're kiss - in' on the porch swing.___   Oh, ___ my lit - tle

sweet   thing. _____

Yeah, I

know I'm gon-na see you first thing to-mor-row, but I just could-n't wait, so I had to bor-row Un-cle

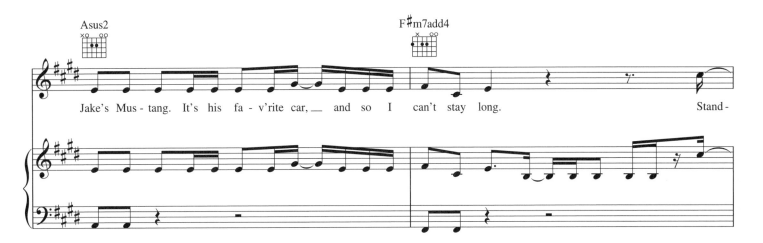

Jake's Mus-tang. It's his fa-v'rite car, __ and so I can't stay long. Stand-

ing here feel-in' like a love-struck Ro - me - o. __ All I wan-na do is hold you close __ and steal a

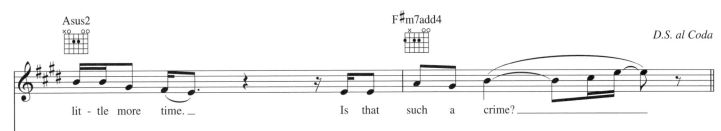

D.S. al Coda

lit - tle more time. __ Is that such a crime? _____

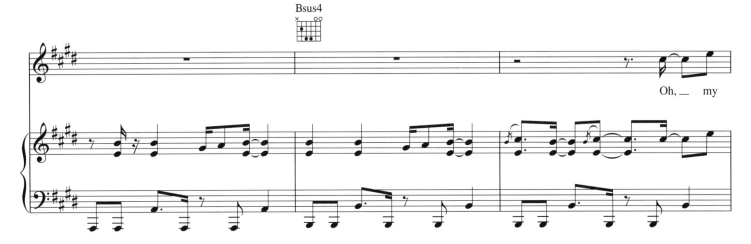

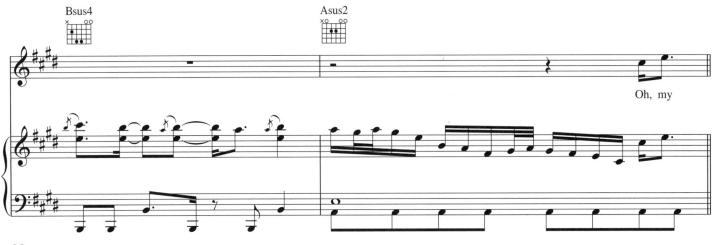

sleep - ing.   'Cause you know I need __ you and there's no   way   I'll be

leav - in'   till we're kiss - in' on the porch swing. __   Oh, __ my lit - tle

sweet thing. __
(Sing 1st time only)

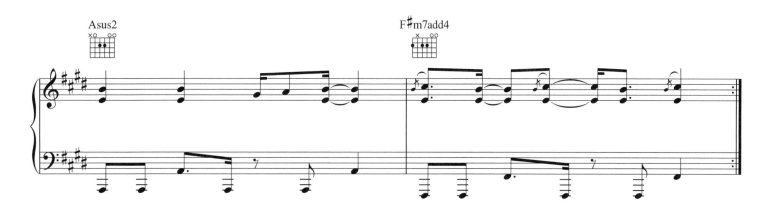

'Til Summer Comes Around

Words and Music by
Monty Powell and Keith Urban

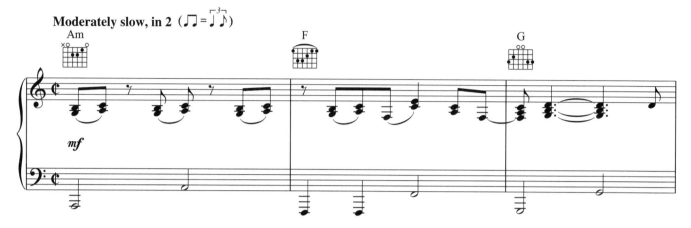

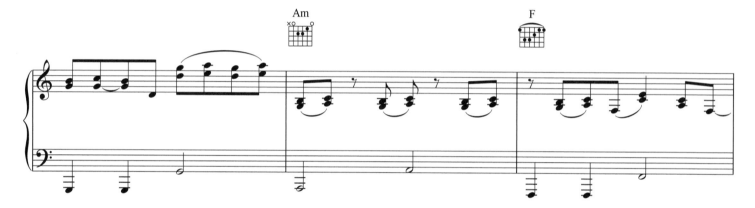

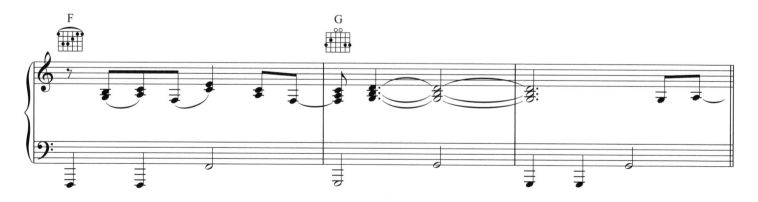

An - oth - er long sum - mer's come and _____ gone.
I got a job work - ing at the old park _____ pier,

I don't know why _____ it al - ways _____ ends _____
and ev - 'ry sum - mer now _____ for _____ five _____

_____ this way. _____ The board - walk's
_____ long years _____ I grease the gears, fix the lights,

qui - et and the car - ni - val rides _____
tight - en bolts, straight - en the tracks, _____

are as emp-ty as my bro-ken heart _____ to - night. _____
and I count the days 'til you just heart might _____ come back. _____

_____ But I } close my eyes _____ and one
_____ And then I } close my eyes _____ and one

more time we're spin-ning a - round _____ and you're hold-ing on _____

tight - ly. The words came out; _____ I kissed your mouth. No Fourth _____

of Ju - ly ___ has ev - er burned so ___ bright - ly. You

had to go; ___ I un - der - stand. But you prom - ised you'd be back a - gain, ___
But you swore ___ that you'd be back a - gain, ___

and so I wan - der 'round this town ___
and so I'm fro - zen in this town ___

1.

'til sum - mer comes ___ a - round. ___
'til

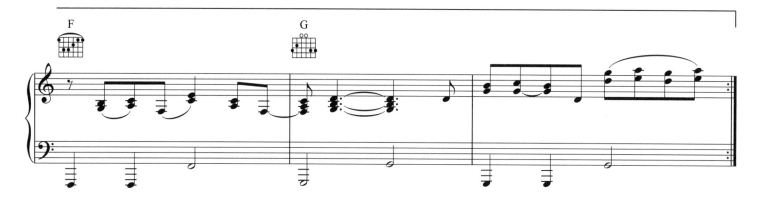

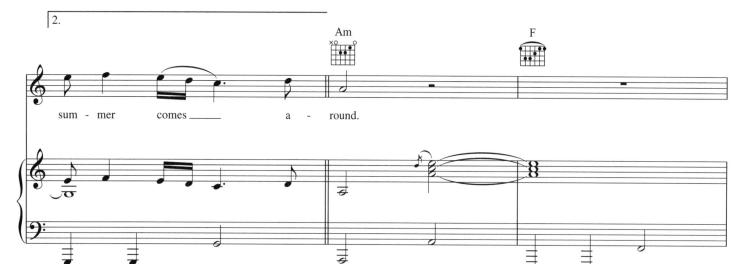

sum - mer comes _____ a - round.

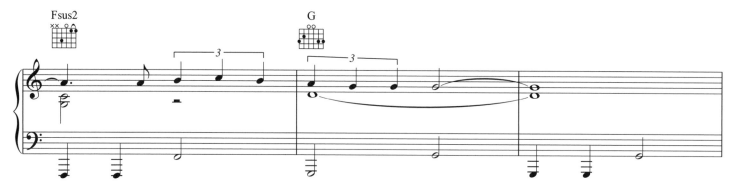

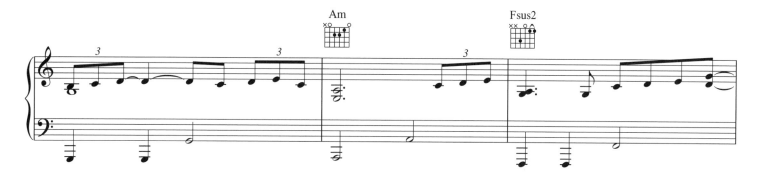

Oh, _____ and I close my eyes __ and you

and I are stuck on the Fer - ris wheel, rock - in' with the mo - tion. And

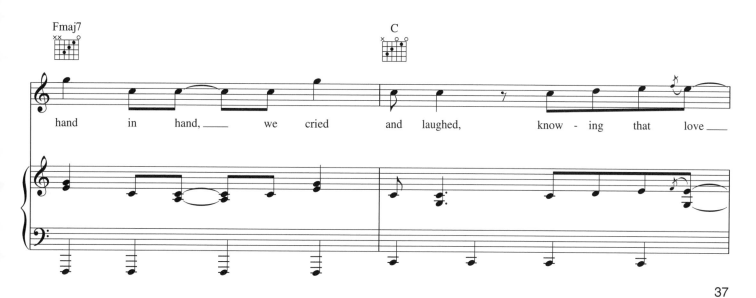

hand in hand, ___ we cried and laughed, know - ing that love ___

be - longed to us, girl, if on - ly for a mo - ment. And "Ba - by, I'll____ be back

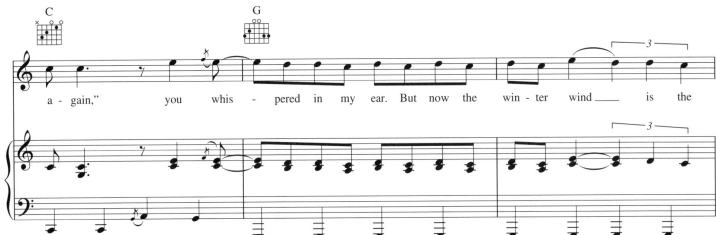

a - gain," you whis - pered in my ear. But now the win - ter wind____ is the

on - ly sound,____

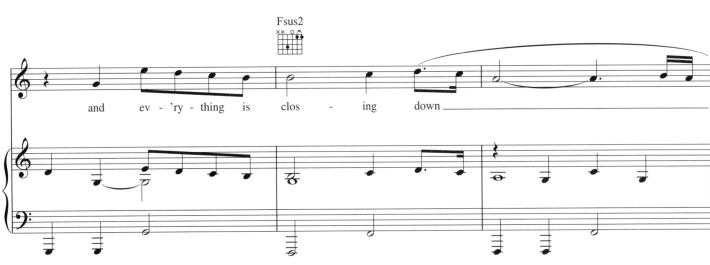

and ev - 'ry - thing is clos - ing down____

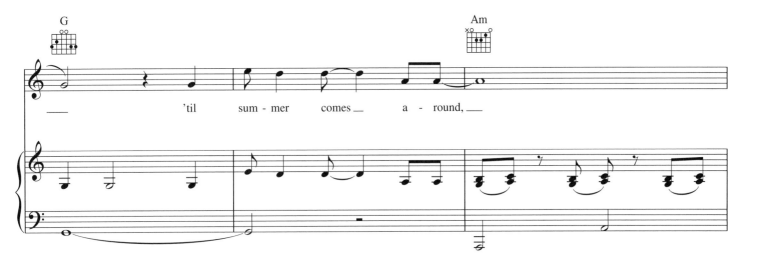

'til sum - mer comes __ a - round, __

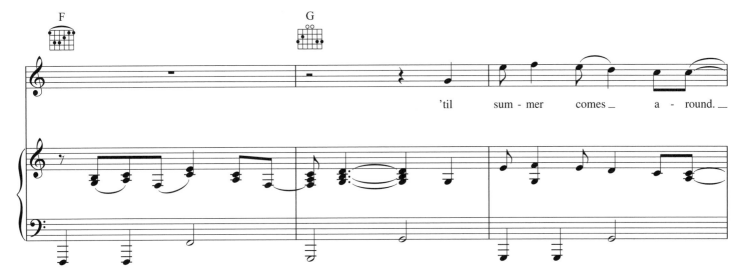

'til sum - mer comes __ a - round. __

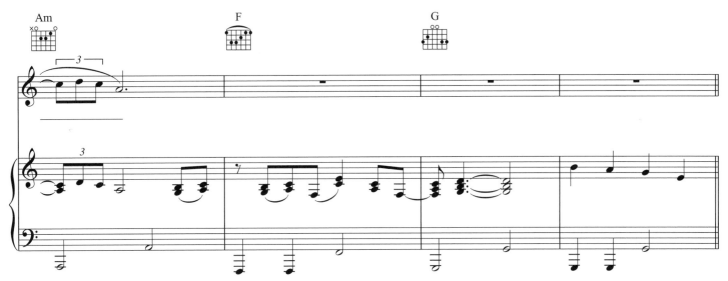

Repeat and fade

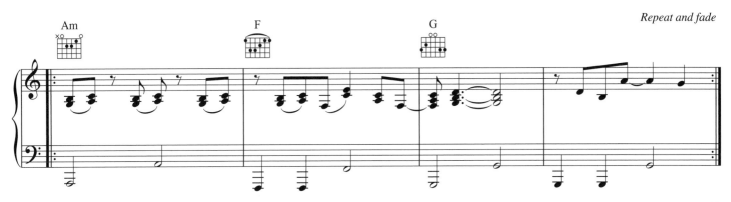

39

My Heart Is Open

Words and Music by
John Shanks and Keith Urban

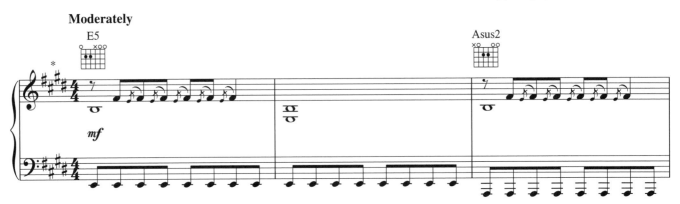

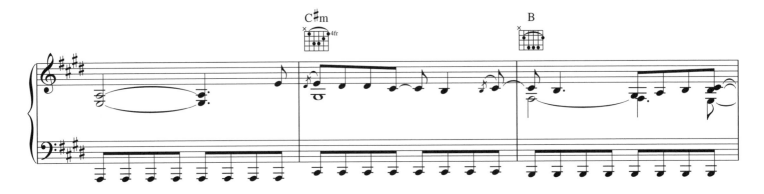

I thought I was do - in' al - right   be - in' a-

*Recorded a half step lower.

lone.

I swore I'd nev-er let ____ some-bod-y get close

a - gain.

I was nev-er gon-na

let ____ my guard ____ down,

not for an-y-one.

But there's a light in your eyes ____ and it's got ____ me mov-

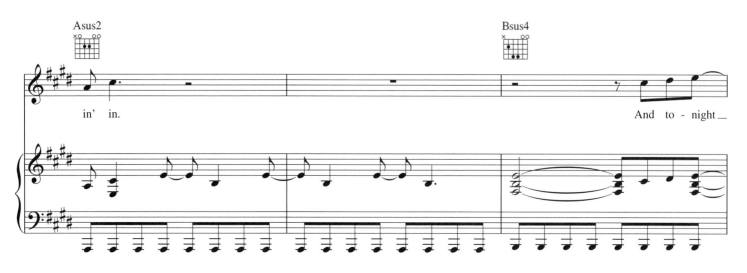

Asus2　　　　　　　　　　　　Bsus4

in' in.　　　　　　　　　　　　　　　　　　　　　　　　　And to - night ___

B　　　　　　　　　Asus2　　　　　　　　F#m7add4

___ these ___ walls ___ are ___ all _____ com - ing down.　And my heart is o-

℅ E　　　　　　　　　　　　　　　　　　　　　　Asus2

pen.　　　　　　　I'm let - tin' you ___ in

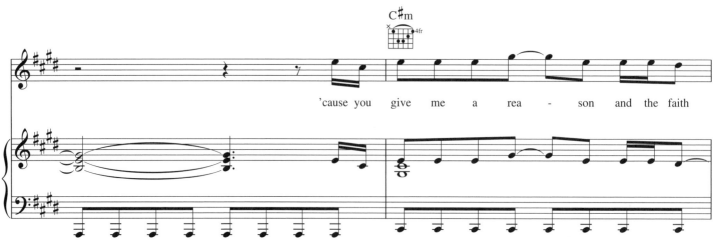

C#m

'cause you give me a rea - son and the faith

pen. ___

E5   Asus2

E5

These days it seems like ev - 'ry-bod - y's just __

Asus2   C#m7

___ walk - ing a - way   like there's no for - ev -

B   Asus2

er and love ___ is just a game. ___   But don't you know __

that you can be - lieve _____ me when I _____ say _____

D.S. al Coda

that I'm your man? And my heart is o

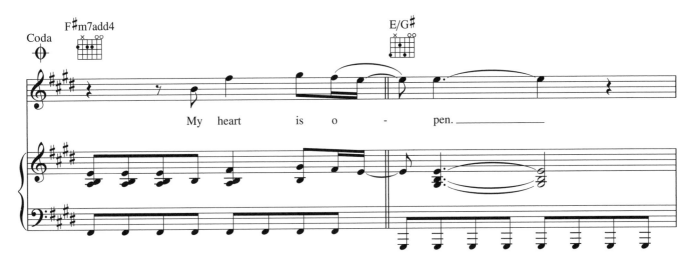

My heart is o - pen. _____

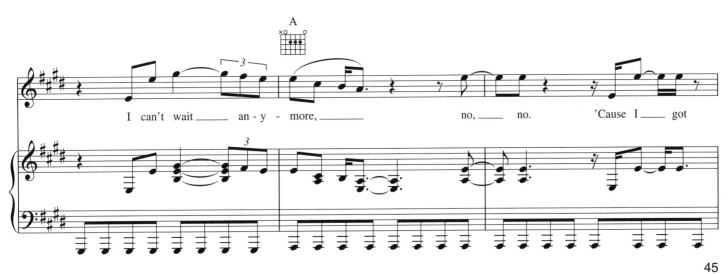

I can't wait _____ an - y - more, _____ no, _____ no. 'Cause I _____ got

F#m

noth - ing left __ to prove, __ and I got so much love __ for you. __ That's why __ I'm

B

tear - ing out the walls __ and, ba - by, I'm kick - ing down the doors. _____

E5   Asus2

C#m   B

Ooh, _ ooh, ooh, _ ooh, yeah. Yeah, _ my heart is o -

pen. _____ O - pen, ooh. _____

_____ My heart is o - pen. _____

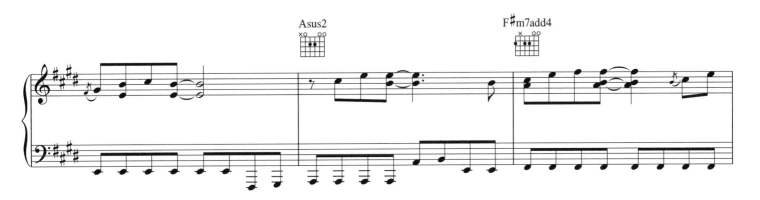

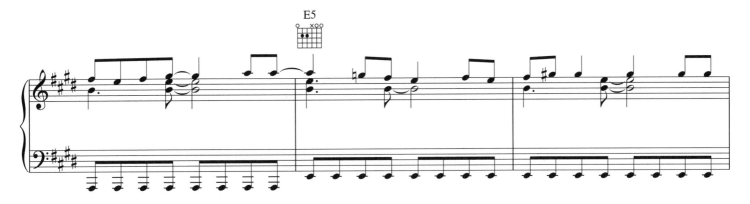

Repeat and fade

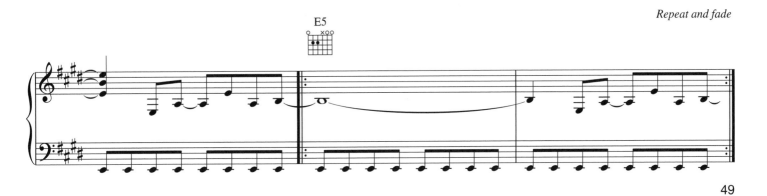

49

Hit the Ground Runnin'
(I Hit the Ground)

Words and Music by
Tony Martin, Mark Nesler and Jerry Flowers

cry - in'. I would-n't sit home a-lone won-d'rin' where I went __ wrong. I'd be
up, __ like some pret-ty red flow-ers and a store - bought __ card that

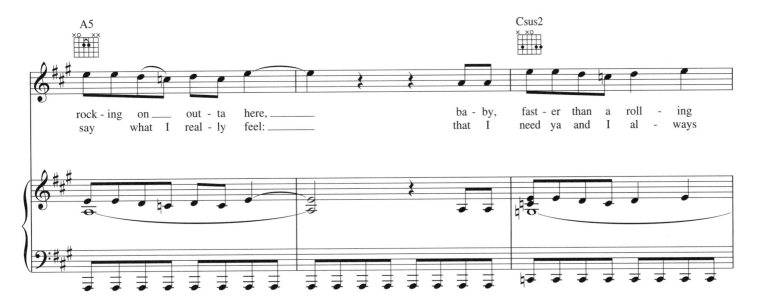

rock - ing on __ out-ta here, _____ ba - by, fast-er than a roll - ing
say what I real -ly feel: _____ that I need ya and I al - ways

tear. __ Ain't no grass gon-na grow un-der me when you're __ gone, no.
will, __ and the three lit-tle words that used to come __ hard. Then I'd

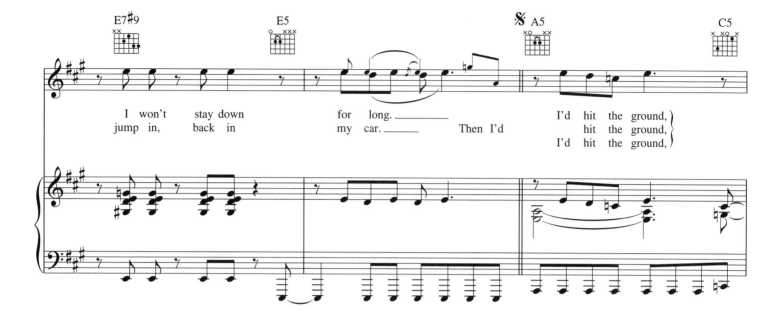

I won't stay down for long. ____ I'd hit the ground,
jump in, back in my car. ____ Then I'd hit the ground,
I'd hit the ground,

I'd hit the ground run-nin'. I know ex-act-ly ____ what I'd do, (hon-ey.)
(hon-ey.)
(sug-ar.)

I'd hit the ground, I'd hit the ground run-nin', I'd hit the ground run-nin'

I'd hit the ground _ run-nin' af - ter _ you. Yes, I would. _

So, if you

got - ta go, _ ba - by, I _ won't stop _ you. _ Mm. _

And _ I won't sit a - round _ and _ miss you, _

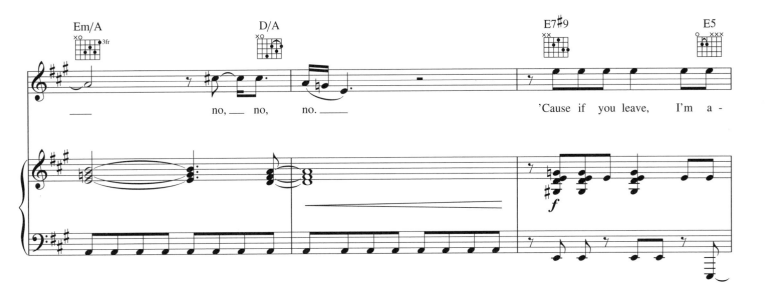

no, __ no, __ no. __ 'Cause if you leave, I'm a-

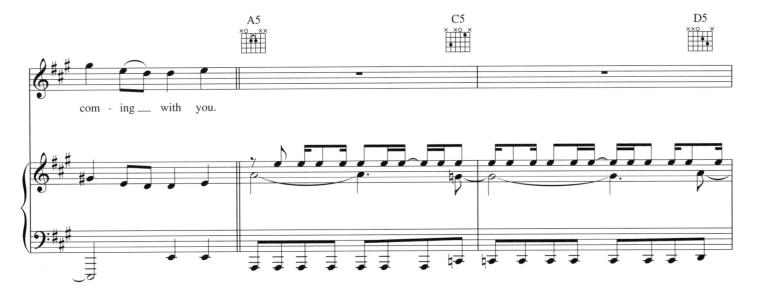

com - ing __ with you.

Coda

af - ter ___ you.   There ain't no doubt;   I ain't that proud. __

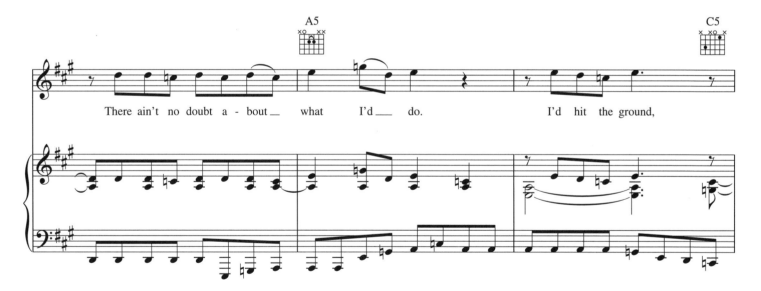

There ain't no doubt a - bout __ what I'd __ do.   I'd hit the ground,

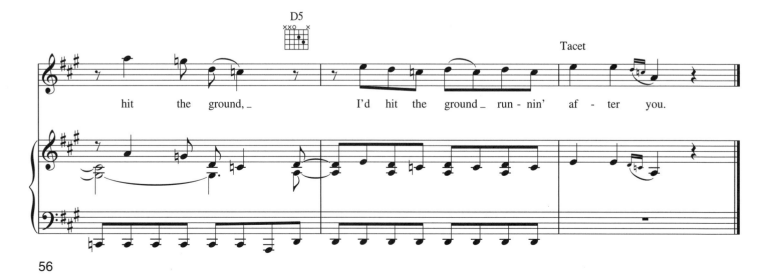

hit   the ground, _   I'd hit the ground _ run - nin' af - ter you.

Only You Can Love Me This Way

Words and Music by
Steve McEwan and John Reid

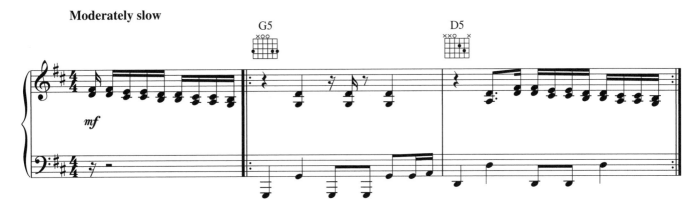

Well, I know there's __ a rea - son,

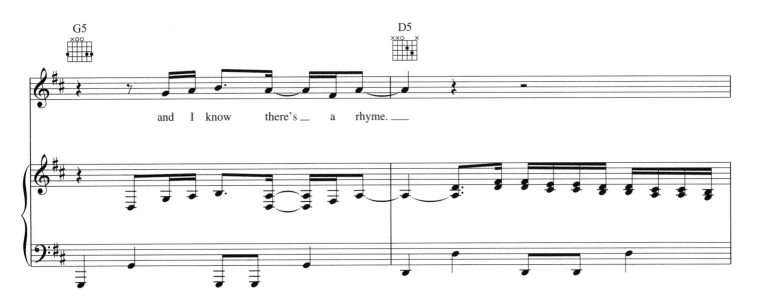

and I know there's __ a rhyme. __

close to you, could ev - er _____ take your place, _____

_____ 'cause on - ly you can love _____ me _____ this way. _____

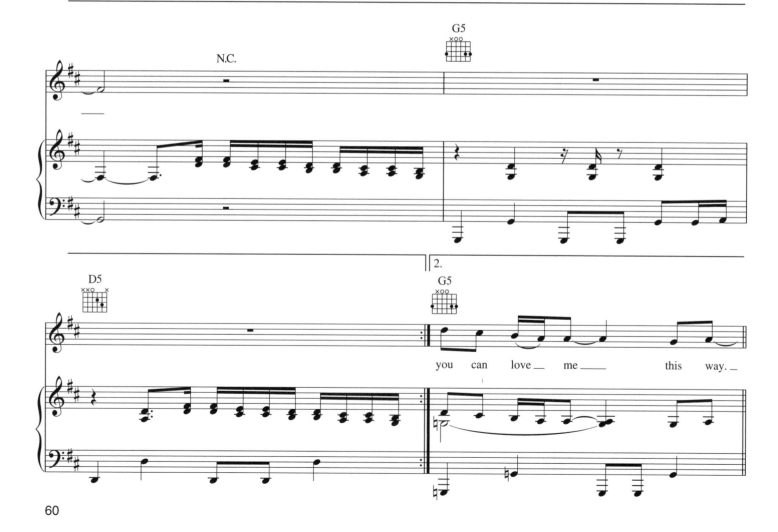

you can love _____ me _____ this way. _____

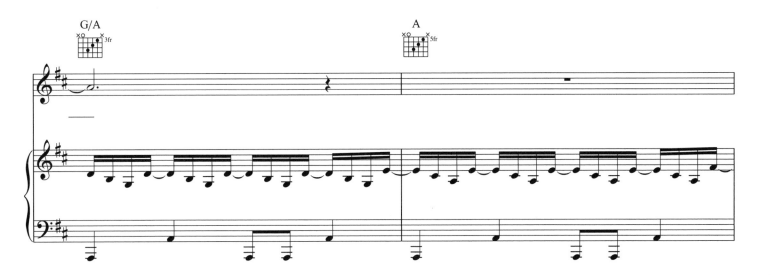

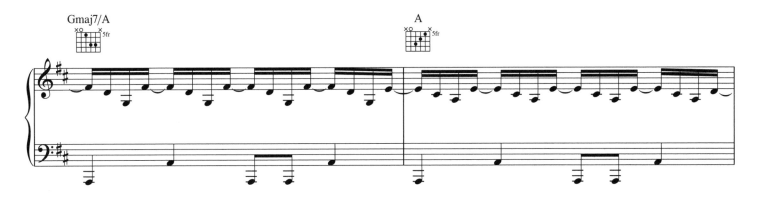

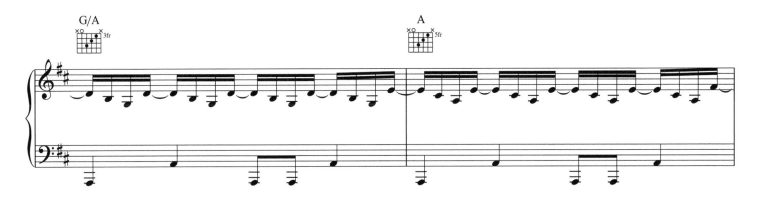

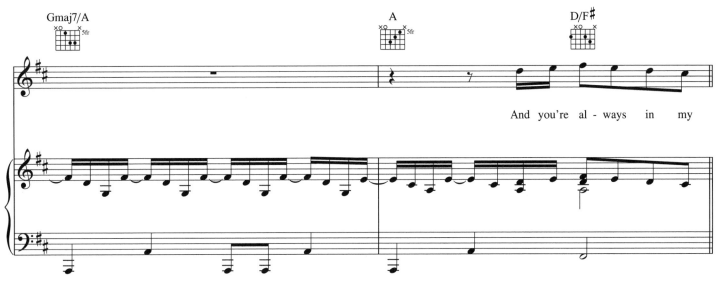

And you're al - ways in my

heart, you're al - ways on my ___ mind. And when it all be - comes too

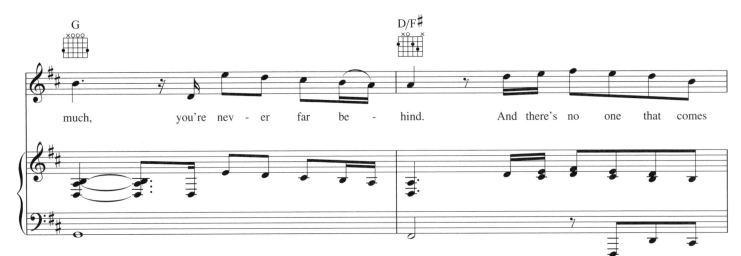

much, you're nev - er far be - hind. And there's no one that comes

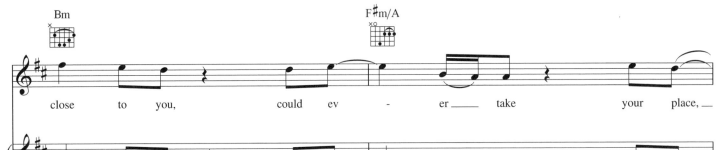

close to you, could ev - er ___ take your place, ___

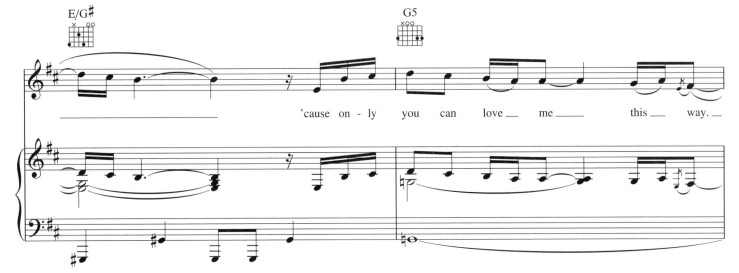

___ 'cause on - ly you can love ___ me ___ this ___ way. ___

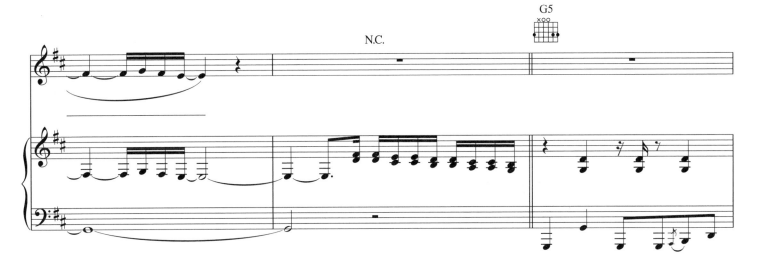

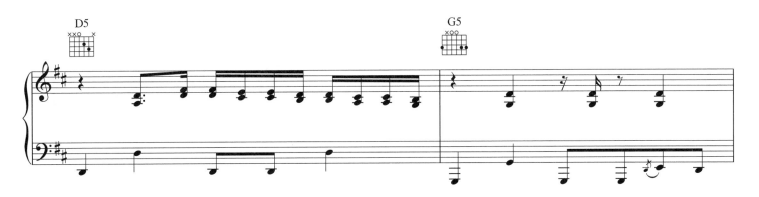

On - ly you can love me this

way.

Standing Right in Front of You

Words and Music by
Rick Nowels and Keith Urban

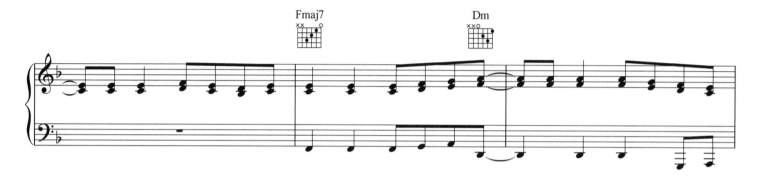

Out on the street cor - ner, just like ev - er - y morn - ing, I sit

*Recorded a half step higher.

here and ___ watch ___ you ___ walk ___ my ___ way. ___ And e - ven though ___

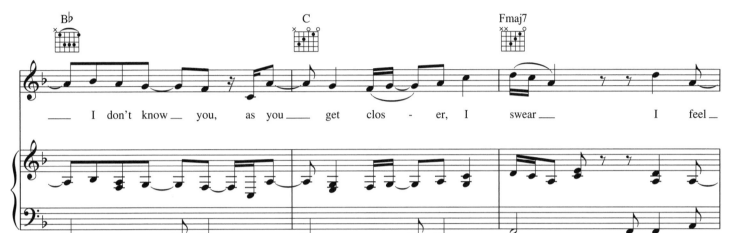

___ I don't know ___ you, as you ___ get clos - er, I swear ___ I feel ___

___ my ___ heart ___ start rac - ing and ach - ing. And may - be it's

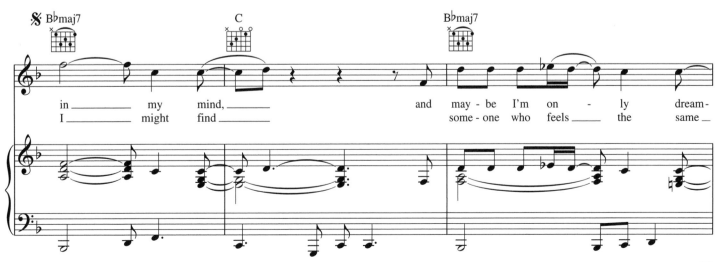

in _____ my mind, _____ and may - be I'm on - ly dream -
I _____ might find _____ some - one who feels ____ the same ___

ing, but I swear you catch _____ my eye _____ as you walk _____
_____ way, some-one to share _____ my life _____ on this beau-

_____ on by. _____ Oh, why _____ you got-ta leave me so blue? _____
ti - ful ride. _____ To - geth - er, we could see it all through. _____

Ba - by, why can't you see _____ that I'm _____ the on - ly one for _____

you? _____ You can search _____ the world _____ o - ver; you'd

never find an-oth-er so true._____ 'Cause if you're looking for love,__ I'm stand-ing right in front of you. I bet your (Stand-ing right in front of you.) heart, like mine,__ has been bro-ken by some-one we nev-

er should-'ve giv-en it to. Oh,___ no.___ So we put___

___ up a wall___ to keep___ from___ fall - ing so hard.___ It's so

D.S. al Coda

sad ___ 'cause there's such___ good love___ in - side,___ and I've been hop-ing that

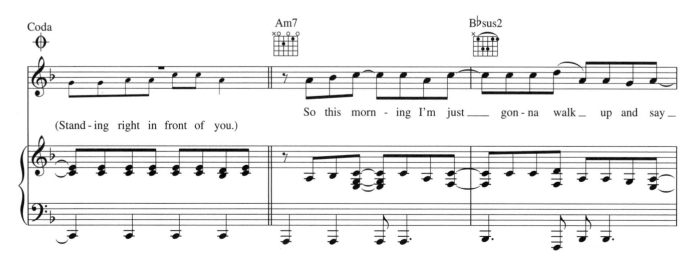

So this morn - ing I'm just___ gon-na walk___ up and say___

(Stand - ing right in front of you.)

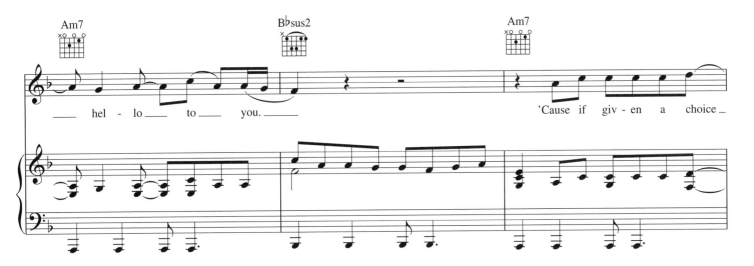

hel - lo __ to __ you. __ 'Cause if giv - en a choice __

__ be - tween love and __ be - ing a - lone, I know __ which one, __ I know __

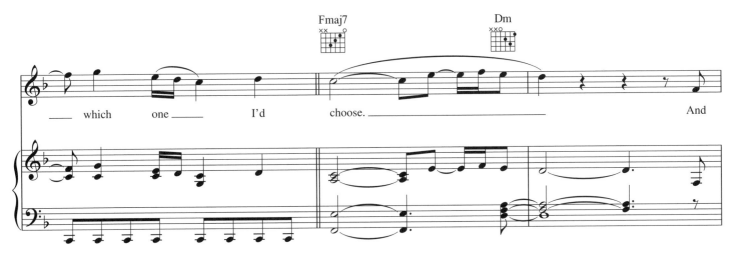

__ which one __ I'd choose. __ And

gim - me a chance; I'd be __ a bet - ter man for you. __ I be -

lieve I would. And o-pen your heart, __ girl; let _____ me make your dreams __ come true. __

You can search __ the world __ o - ver, but

I can take it to the moon. _____ 'Cause if you're

look - ing for love, __ I'm stand - ing right in front of you.

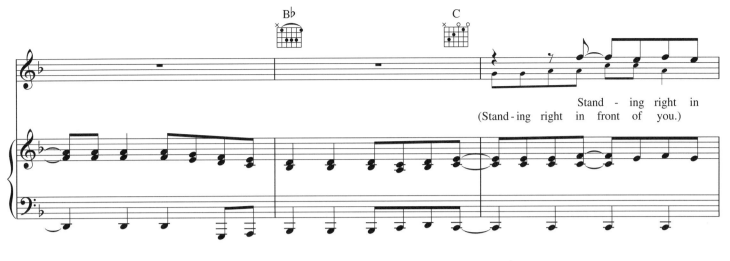

Stand - ing right in
(Stand-ing right in front of you.)

front of you. ___ Woh, _____ woh, __ woh. And o - pen your eyes __ now.

Yeah, yeah. __ Just give me a chance, __ ba - by.
(Stand-ing right in front of you.)

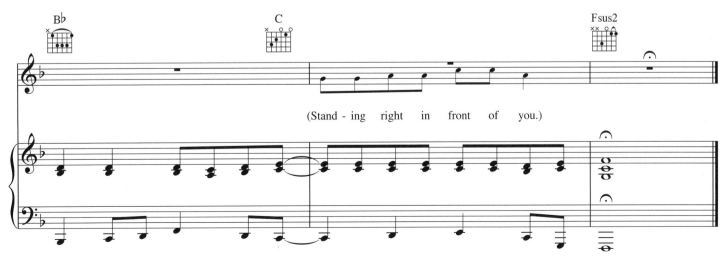

(Stand-ing right in front of you.)

Why's It Feel So Long

Words and Music by
Keith Urban

Moderate Country/Rock

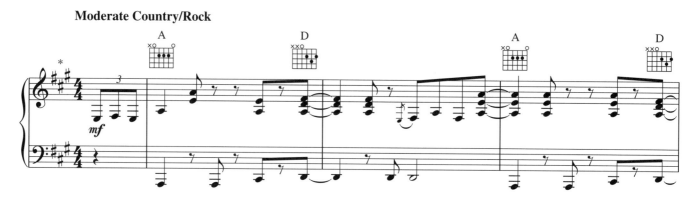

I just kissed you good - bye ___
I've nev - er loved an -

___ a half an hour a - go. ___ I know you're driv -
y - one like I loved you. ___ So when you're not a - round, ___

*Recorded a half step lower.

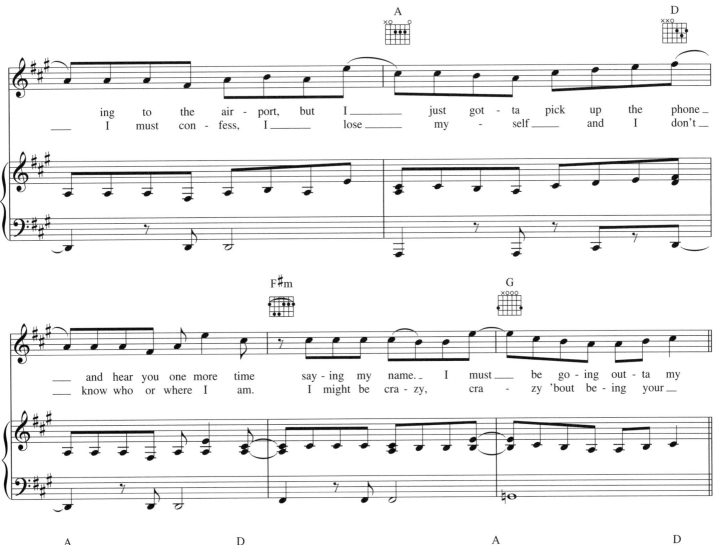

ing to the air - port, but I _____ just got - ta pick up the phone _
_ I must con - fess, I _____ lose _____ my - self _____ and I don't _

_ and hear you one more time _____ say - ing my name. _ I must _____ be go - ing out - ta my
_ know who or where I am. _____ I might be cra - zy, cra - zy 'bout be - ing your _

mind. } Why's it feel so _____ long _____ since you been _ gone? _ Why's it feel so _____ long? _
man. }

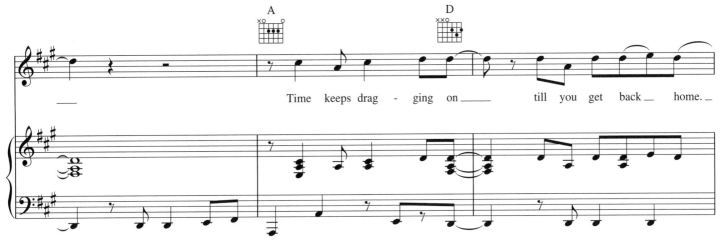

Time keeps drag - ging on _____ till you get back _ home. _

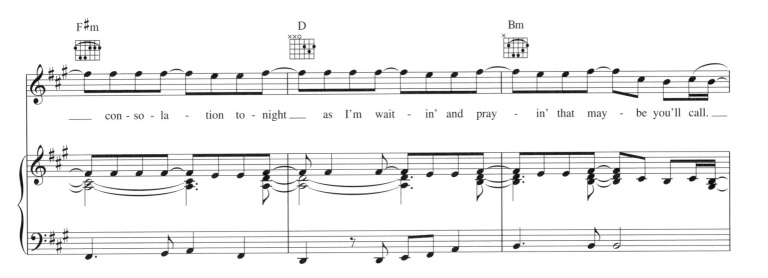

con-so-la-tion to-night ___ as I'm wait-in' and pray – in' that may – be you'll call. ___

___ Call ___ me, call ___ me, ba – by. _____

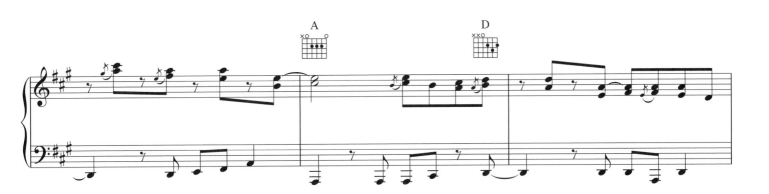

Tell me now: Why's it feel so ___ long ___ since you been ___ gone? ___

___ Why's it feel so ___ long? ___

{ Time keeps drag - ging on ___
{ Time just crawls a - long ___

___ } till you get back ___ home. ___ Why's it feel so ___ long? ___ Oh, ___ oh.

1.

2.

___ I look at my watch, ___ stare at the clock, ___ and they don't move. ___

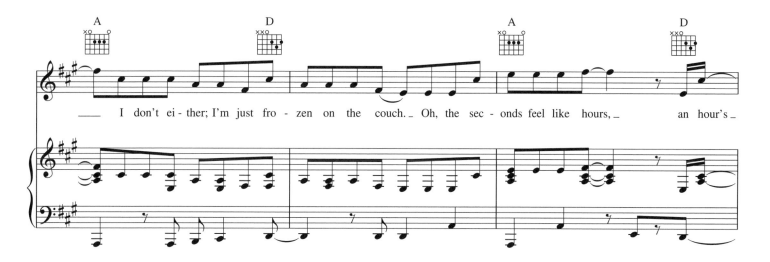

I don't ei - ther; I'm just fro - zen on the couch. Oh, the sec - onds feel like hours, _____ an hour's _____

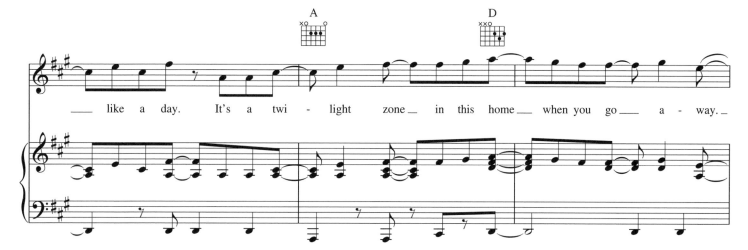

_____ like a day. It's a twi - light zone _____ in this home _____ when you go _____ a - way. _____

_____ Please, _____ don't go a - way. _____ Ooh, _____

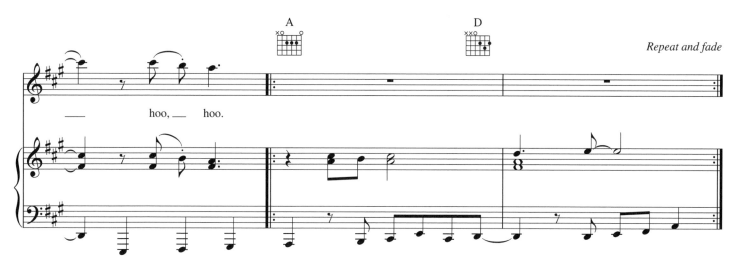

_____ hoo, _____ hoo.

Repeat and fade

I'm In

Words and Music by
Radney Foster and Georgia Middleman

Moderately fast

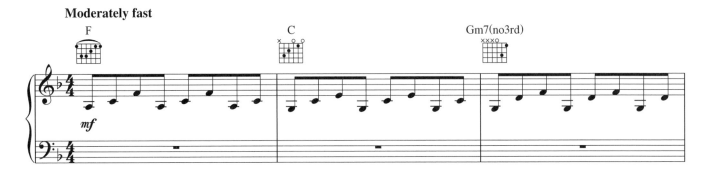

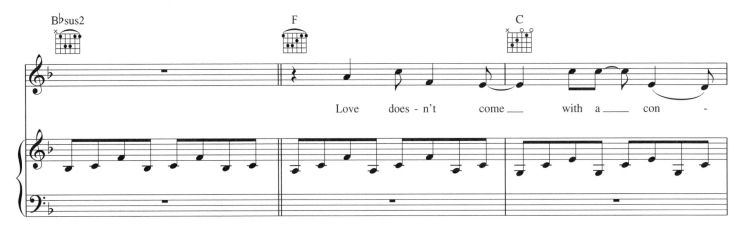

Love does-n't come ___ with a ___ con -

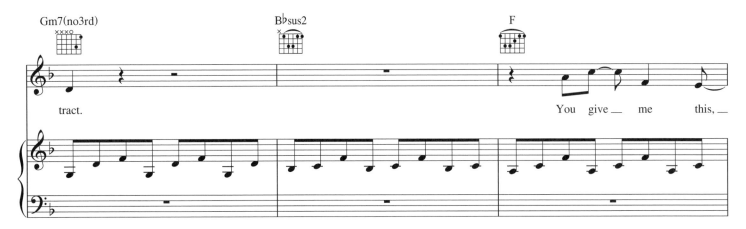

tract. You give ___ me this, ___

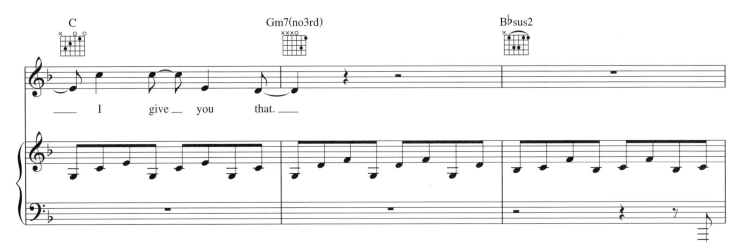

___ I give ___ you that. ___

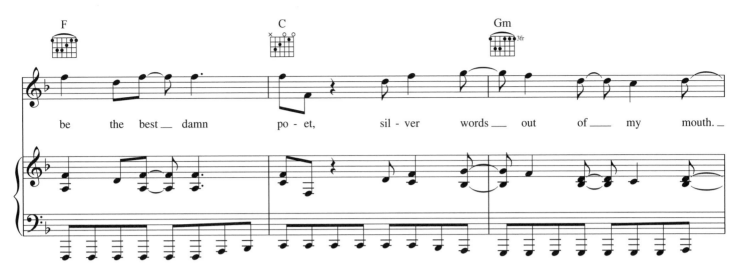

be   the   best ___ damn   po - et,   sil - ver   words ___ out   of ___ my   mouth. ___

___   Well,   my   words ___ might   not ___ be   mag - ic,   but   they   cut ___

___   straight   to ___ the   truth. ___   So   if   you   need ___ a

To Coda II   *To Coda I*

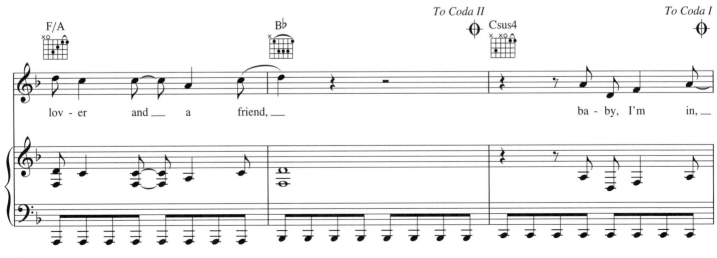

lov - er   and ___ a   friend, ___   ba - by,   I'm   in, ___

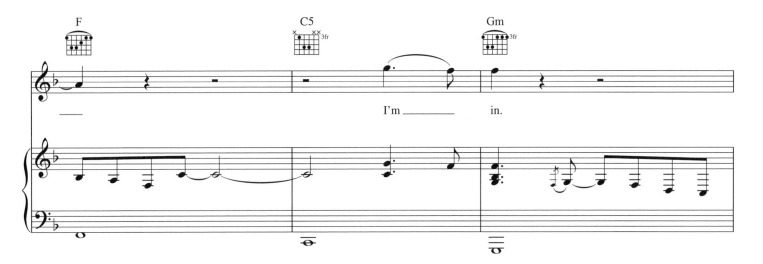

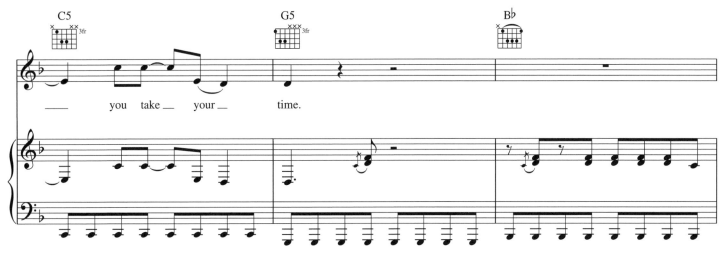

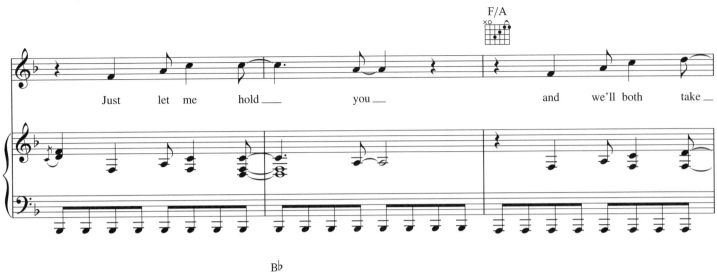

Just let me hold ___ you ___ and we'll both take ___

___ that leap ___ of ___ faith. ___ It's like ___ I told ___ you: there's ___ no guar-

D.S. al Coda I

an - tees ___ when you feel ___ this way. ___ If I

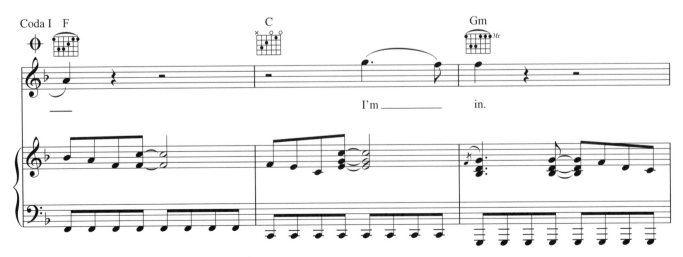

I'm ___ in.

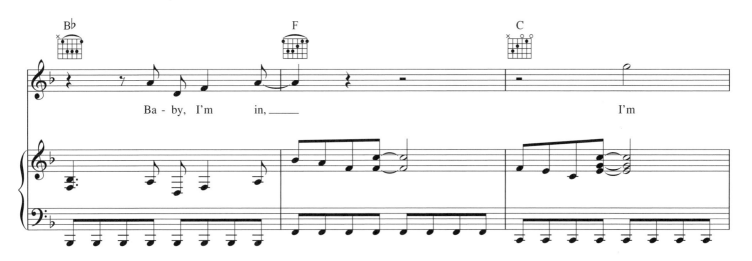

Ba - by, I'm in, _____ I'm

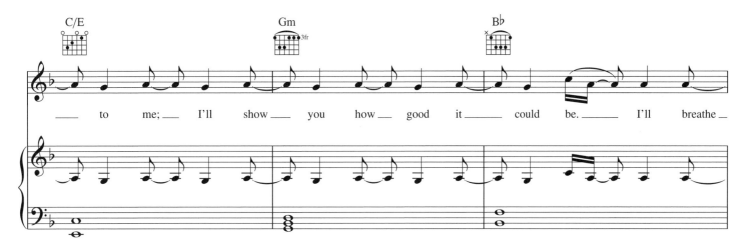

in. _____ Ba - by, come _ here next _

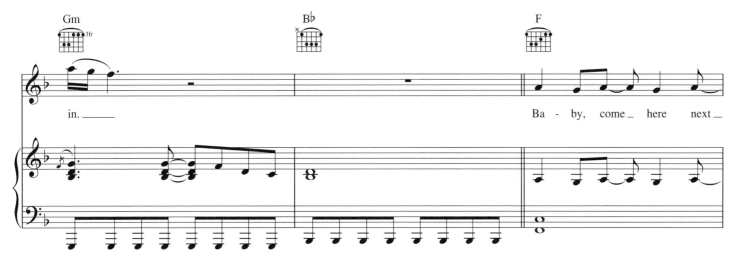

_____ to me; _ I'll show _ you how _ good it _____ could be. _____ I'll breathe _

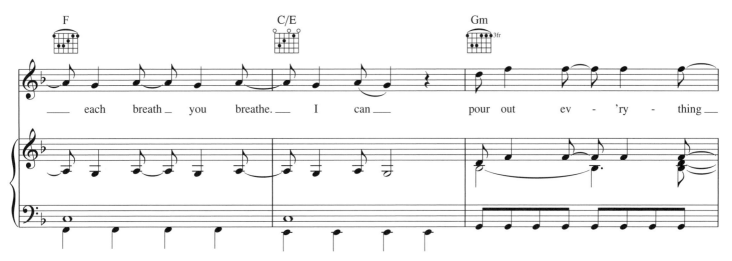

_____ each breath _ you breathe. _ I can _ pour out ev - 'ry - thing _

D.S. al Coda II

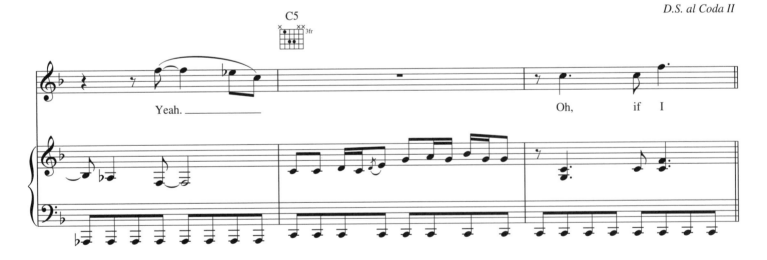

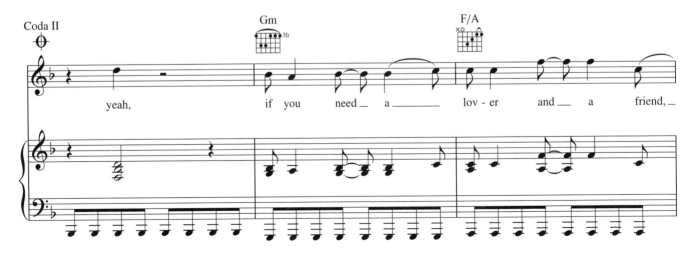

84

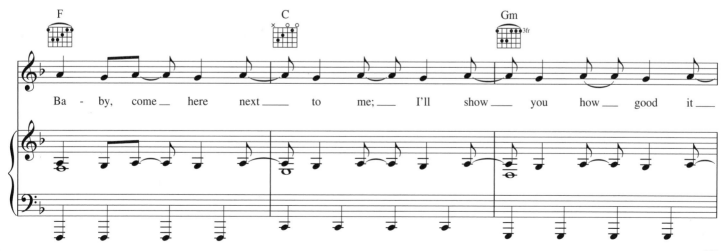

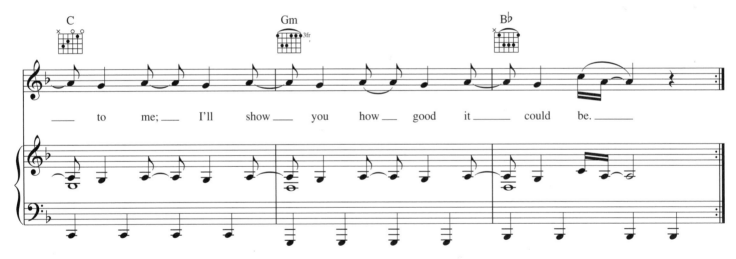

Thank You

Words and Music by
Rick Nowels and Keith Urban

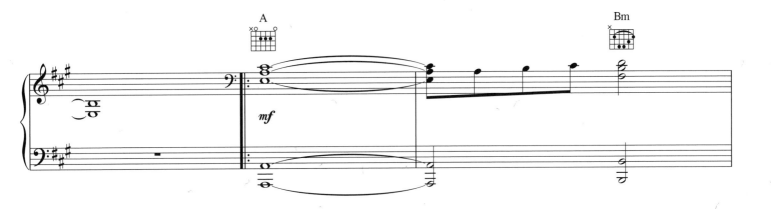

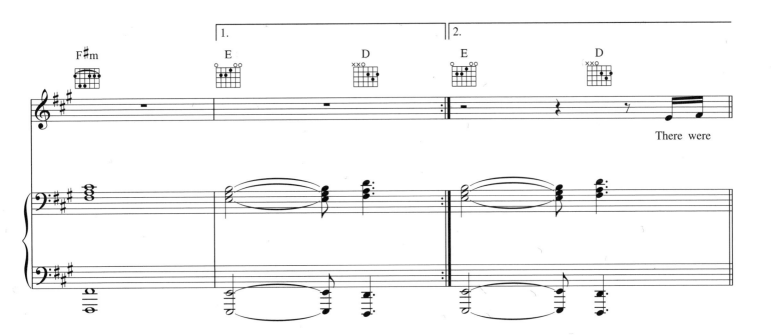

There were

some-thing so fa-mil-iar a-bout the way you said— my name.— And the

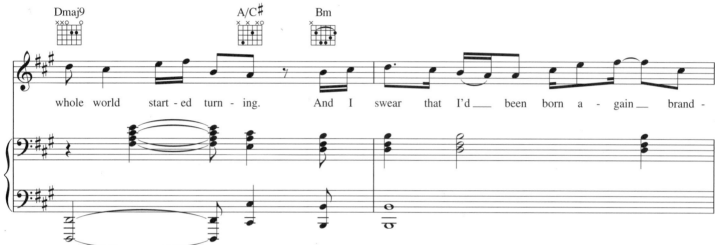

whole world start-ed turn-ing. And I swear that I'd— been born a-gain— brand-

D.S. al Coda

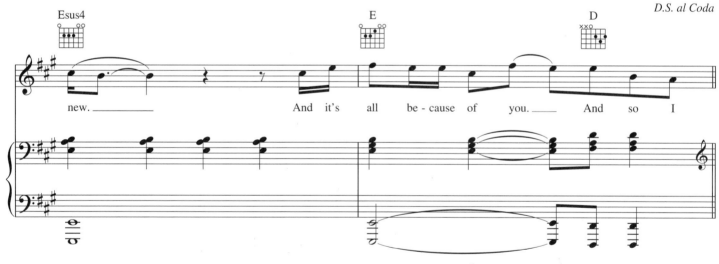

new.———— And it's all be-cause of you.— And so I

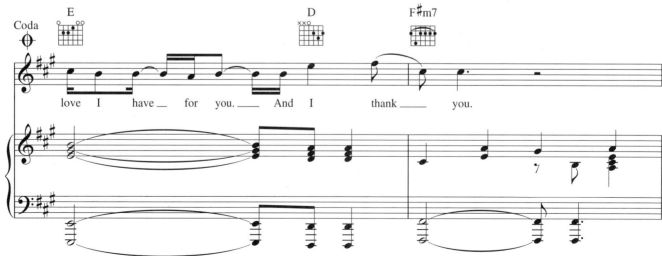

love I have— for you.— And I thank— you.

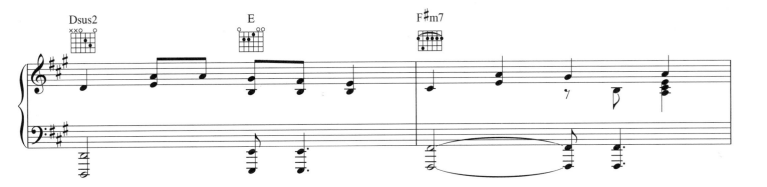

And I've seen so man-y things that

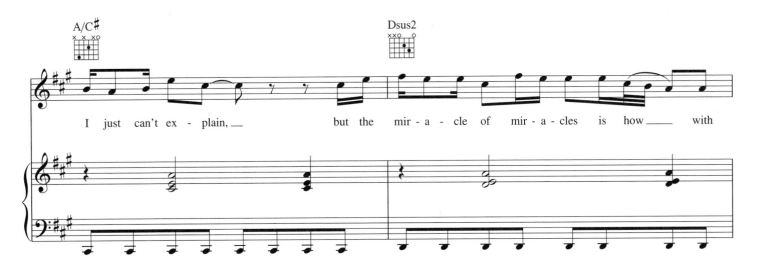

I just can't ex-plain, ___ but the mir-a-cle of mir-a-cles is how ___ with

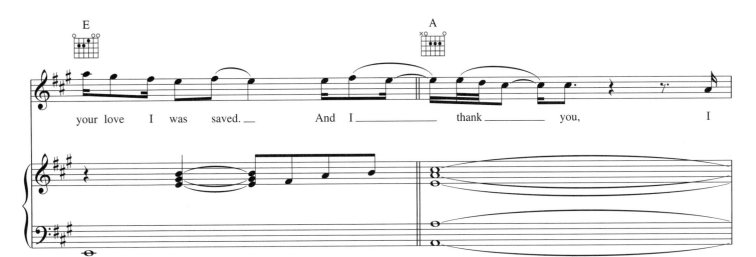

your love I was saved. ___ And I ___ thank ___ you, I

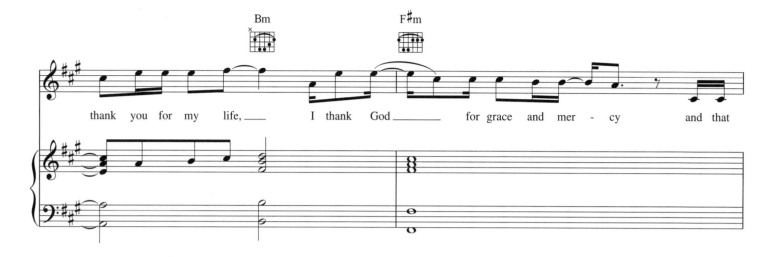

thank you for my life, ___ I thank God ___ for grace and mer - cy ___ and that

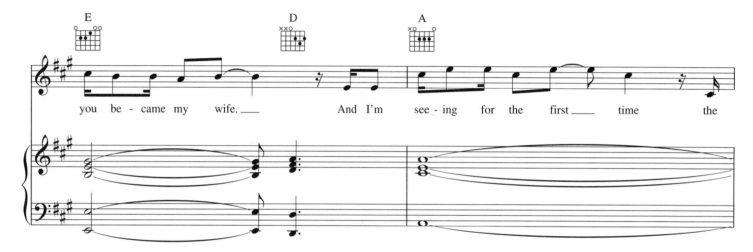

you be - came my wife. ___ And I'm see - ing for the first ___ time the

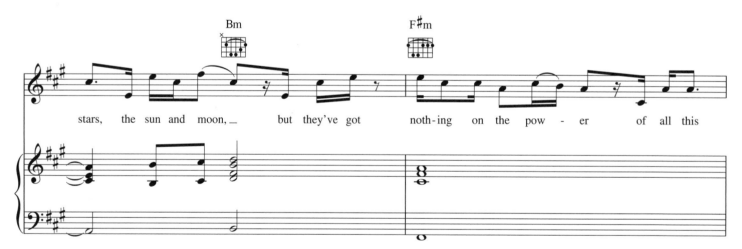

stars, the sun and moon, ___ but they've got noth-ing on the pow - er of all this

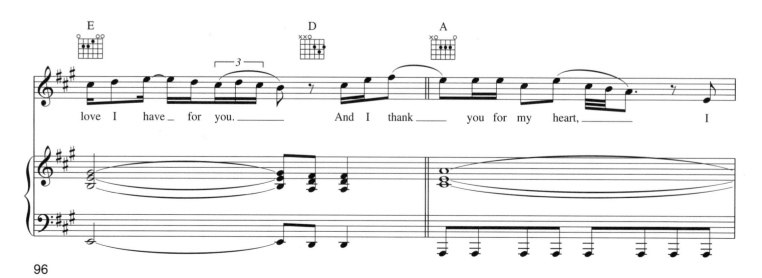

love I have _ for you. ___ And I thank ___ you for my heart, ___ I

Ooh, ___ yes, I do. ___ Oh, ___

___ don't you know ___ that I ___ thank ___ you. ___

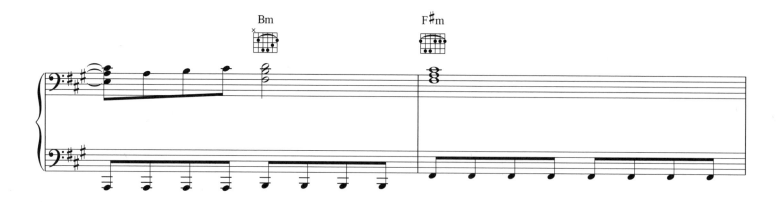

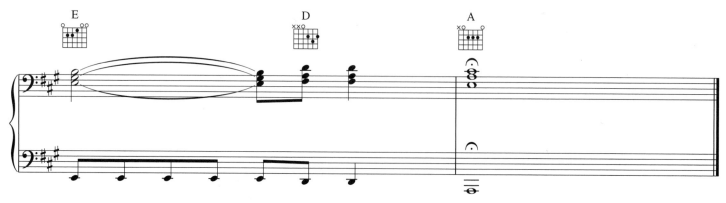

great songs series

This legendary series has delighted players and performers for generations.

Great Songs of the Fifties

Features rock, pop, country, Broadway and movie tunes, including: All Shook Up • At the Hop • Blue Suede Shoes • Dream Lover • Fly Me to the Moon • Kansas City • Love Me Tender • Misty • Peggy Sue • Rock Around the Clock • Sea of Love • Sixteen Tons • Take the "A" Train • Wonderful! Wonderful! • and more. Includes an introduction by award-winning journalist Bruce Pollock.
02500323 P/V/G...$16.95

Great Songs of the Sixties, Vol. 1 – Revised

The updated version of this classic book includes 80 faves from the 1960s: Angel of the Morning • Bridge over Troubled Water • Cabaret • Different Drum • Do You Believe in Magic • Eve of Destruction • Monday, Monday • Spinning Wheel • Walk on By • and more.
02509902 P/V/G...$19.95

Great Songs of the Sixties, Vol. 2 – Revised

61 more '60s hits: California Dreamin' • Crying • For Once in My Life • Honey • Little Green Apples • MacArthur Park • Me and Bobby McGee • Nowhere Man • Piece of My Heart • Sugar, Sugar • You Made Me So Very Happy • and more.
02509904 P/V/G...$19.95

Great Songs of the Seventies, Vol. 1 – Revised

This super collection of 70 big hits from the '70s includes: After the Love Has Gone • Afternoon Delight • Annie's Song • Band on the Run • Cold as Ice • FM • Imagine • It's Too Late • Layla • Let It Be • Maggie May • Piano Man • Shelter from the Storm • Superstar • Sweet Baby James • Time in a Bottle • The Way We Were • and more.
02509917 P/V/G...$19.95

Great Songs of the Seventies, Vol. 2

Features 58 outstanding '70s songs in rock, pop, country, Broadway and movie genres: American Woman • The Loco-Motion • My Eyes Adored You • New Kid in Town • Night Fever • Summer Breeze • Tonight's the Night • We Are the Champions • Y.M.C.A. • more. Includes articles by Cherry Lane Music Company founder Milt Okun, and award-winning music journalist Bruce Pollock.
02500322 P/V/G...$19.95

Great Songs of the Eighties – Revised

This edition features 50 songs in rock, pop & country styles, plus hits from Broadway and the movies! Songs: Almost Paradise • Angel of the Morning • Do You Really Want to Hurt Me • Endless Love • Flashdance...What a Feeling • Guilty • Hungry Eyes • (Just Like) Starting Over • Let Love Rule • Missing You • Patience • Through the Years • Time After Time • Total Eclipse of the Heart • and more.
02502125 P/V/G...$18.95

Great Songs of the Nineties

Includes: Achy Breaky Heart • Beautiful in My Eyes • Believe • Black Hole Sun • Black Velvet • Blaze of Glory • Building a Mystery • Crash into Me • Fields of Gold • From a Distance • Glycerine • Here and Now • Hold My Hand • I'll Make Love to You • Ironic • Linger • My Heart Will Go On • Waterfalls • Wonderwall • and more.
02500040 P/V/G...$16.95

Great Songs of Broadway

This fabulous collection of 60 standards includes: Getting to Know You • Hello, Dolly! • The Impossible Dream • Let Me Entertain You • My Favorite Things • My Husband Makes Movies • Oh, What a Beautiful Mornin' • On My Own • People • Tomorrow • Try to Remember • Unusual Way • What I Did for Love • and dozens more, plus an introductory article.
02500615 P/V/G...$19.95

Great Songs of Classic Rock

Nearly 50 of the greatest songs of the rock era, including: Against the Wind • Cold As Ice • Don't Stop Believin' • Feels like the First Time • I Can See for Miles • Maybe I'm Amazed • Minute by Minute • Money • Nights in White Satin • Only the Lonely • Open Arms • Rikki Don't Lose That Number • Rosanna • We Are the Champions • and more.
02500801 P/V/G...$19.95

Great Songs of the Country Era

This volume features 58 country gems, including: Abilene • Afternoon Delight • Amazed • Annie's Song • Blue • Crazy • Elvira • Fly Away • For the Good Times • Friends in Low Places • The Gambler • Hey, Good Lookin' • I Hope You Dance • Thank God I'm a Country Boy • This Kiss • Your Cheatin' Heart • and more.
02500503 P/V/G...$19.95

Great Songs of Folk Music

Nearly 50 of the most popular folk songs of our time, including: Blowin' in the Wind • The House of the Rising Sun • Puff the Magic Dragon • This Land Is Your Land • Time in a Bottle • The Times They Are A-Changin' • The Unicorn • Where Have All the Flowers Gone? • and more.
02500997 P/V/G...$19.95

Great Songs from The Great American Songbook

52 American classics, including: Ain't That a Kick in the Head • As Time Goes By • Come Fly with Me • Georgia on My Mind • I Get a Kick Out of You • I've Got You Under My Skin • The Lady Is a Tramp • Love and Marriage • Mack the Knife • Misty • Over the Rainbow • People • Take the "A" Train • Thanks for the Memory • and more.
02500760 P/V/G...$16.95

Great Songs of the Movies

Nearly 60 of the best songs popularized in the movies, including: Accidentally in Love • Alfie • Almost Paradise • The Rainbow Connection • Somewhere in My Memory • Take My Breath Away (Love Theme) • Three Coins in the Fountain • (I've Had) the Time of My Life • Up Where We Belong • The Way We Were • and more.
02500967 P/V/G...$19.95

Great Songs of the Pop Era

Over 50 hits from the pop era, including: Every Breath You Take • I'm Every Woman • Just the Two of Us • Leaving on a Jet Plane • My Cherie Amour • Raindrops Keep Fallin' on My Head • Time After Time • (I've Had) the Time of My Life • What a Wonderful World • and more.
02500043 Easy Piano.....................................$16.95

Great Songs of the Pop/Rock Era

65 fabulous pop/rock favorites in piano/vocal/guitar format. Includes: Africa • Annie's Song • If • Imagine • Jack and Diane • Lady in Red • Oh, Pretty Woman • Respect • Rock Around the Clock • (Sittin' On) The Dock of the Bay • Tears in Heaven • Time in a Bottle • Yesterday • and more.
02500552 P/V/G...$19.95

Great Songs of the 2000s

Over 50 of the decade's biggest hits so far, including: Accidentally in Love • Breathe (2 AM) • Daughters • Hanging by a Moment • The Middle • The Remedy (I Won't Worry) • Smooth • A Thousand Miles • and more.
02500922 P/V/G...$19.99

Great Songs for Weddings

A beautiful collection of 59 pop standards perfect for wedding ceremonies and receptions, including: Always and Forever • Amazed • Beautiful in My Eyes • Can You Feel the Love Tonight • Endless Love • Love of a Lifetime • Open Arms • Unforgettable • When I Fall in Love • The Wind Beneath My Wings • and more.
02501006 P/V/G...$19.95

Prices, contents, and availability subject to change without notice.

EXCLUSIVELY DISTRIBUTED BY
HAL•LEONARD® CORPORATION
7777 W. BLUEMOUND RD. P.O. BOX 13819 MILWAUKEE, WI 53213

www.cherrylane.com

0409

More Great Piano/Vocal Books

FROM CHERRY LANE

For a complete listing of Cherry Lane titles available,
including contents listings, please visit our web site at

www.cherrylane.com

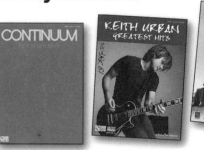